MW01294619

Printed in the USA

French Swearing:
Top 49 French Insults and
How to Use Them
(A Quick and Dirty Guide)

By Francois Martin

Table of Contents

French was the diplomatic language in Europe for hundreds of years, back when men wore tights and women wore hats shaped like dunce caps. If you were a king or important courtier, no matter what country you lived in, you spoke French. It was simply what fancy people did. Because of this, written and formal language in France had to be respectful and correspond to a certain level of expectation depending on the context. However, the French language is (and always has been) rich in many slang expressions and swear words. These are a people who really know how to express themselves in ways that stretch the limits of creativity.

Overall, vulgarity is not accepted in the "serious" areas of life, such as work, politics or even movies productions that are meant to be solemn affairs. Depending your on age and background, swearing around your family might be off-limits, too. And when it comes to your education, notably when you are on school property, you have to watch your mouth.

Entertainment is another story, however; in the recent years the level of vulgarity on TV and in some movies has increased, particularly in Trash-TV, in TV shows, in comedy movies and in humor.

It might have been considered even more inappropriate for women to swear, but the surge of vulgar TV and movies has democratized this effect, particularly with the influence of female humorists who don't hesitate to run their mouths, sometimes more than men.

In family, as a child it's almost always forbidden to swear in the house or in front of the parents, and the adults also try to reciprocate by not swearing in front of the children. Over time, though, depending on the tolerance of the family and on the social and cultural backgrounds, these rules might loosen.

The slang expressions in French have different origins, but a lot of them are inspired by sexual practices or inclinations. Some came from some slang languages as "louchébem" used by Parisian butchers in the first part of the 19th century, or "javanais" who appears in the late 19th century, or more recently the "verlan," originally linked to the hip-hop culture. Today the "verlan" is globally used and understood.

This guide is the perfect companion for your next trip to France; why should you censor yourself simply because you're not speaking your native tongue? In France, anything is possible, and you will want to be able to tell your new French friends exactly how you feel about any given situation.

And it might be useful knowing what others are saying about you!

Insults for the Ladies

As an American, you probably aren't too familiar with many French women. Most likely, your interaction with French women is limited to watching them in movies. Eva Green, Marion Cotillard, Sophie Marceau and Lea Seydoux are some of the most popular actresses working today, and while if it's hard to imagine yourself flinging any of these curse words their way, try to picture them saying the words instead. Much better, right? Channel your inner Eva or Marion as you let these feminine insults roll off your tongue. Maybe add a smoldering eye into the mix and *voila* — you're ready to take down any French person who gives you some of that famous attitude.

1. Tart: *Poufiasse*

Sure, "tart" isn't the worst thing you can all a woman, but it's not exactly a compliment either, connoting as it does a certain kind of sartorial style and the behavior to match. Who knows, thought — you might see someone who looks tart-like while you're out enjoying the vibrant French nightlife; or, conversely, perhaps you'll be the one hearing someone say "Poufiasse!" as you head into a club.

Example: I think I've still seen him with some tart last night.

Je pense l'avoir encore aperçu avec une poufiasse quelconque hier soir.

2. Grumpy cow: *Grognasse*

The nice thing about "grumpy cow" is that no matter how young and beautiful the woman you're speaking to, this insult will immediately rattle her. No one wants to be compared to the bovine creatures who linger in green pastures, chewing their cud with immovable placidity. And a dash of grumpiness is even worse. Well, if you kick out at the person who called you a "grognasse," at least you're staying in theme.

Example: She is still grumbling, this one?! What a grumpy cow!

Elle est encore en train de râler?! Quelle grognasse!

3. Hooker/Whore: *Pute*

With their looser approach to sexuality in France, it might be slightly more difficult to elicit a "Pute!" response out of the French, but that doesn't mean you should go out of your way to earn it. On the other hand, if that cute guy you were eyeing suddenly takes up with someone else, you know what to mutter under your breath when they walk by, looking happy.

Example: Why is it Jane knows so many men? Because she's a whore!

Pourquoi Stéphanie connaît autant d'hommes? Parce que c'est une pute!

4. Bitch/slut: *Salope*

When women really into an argument, "bitch" and "slut" tend to come out (as the gloves come off). There is something about attacking a woman's character — regardless of whether or not her character actually fits the bill — that is oh-so-satisfying. Even better? Surprising a male opponent with a casual "At least I'm not a little bitch like you!" Just try not to smile and ruin the effect.

Example: You're just willing to do anything for your interest!
              You're a bitch!

              *Tu es juste prête à tout pour ton intérêt! Tu n'es
              qu'une salope!*

5. Complete moron/Dizzy bitch: *Abruti fini*

Think of "abruti fini" as applicable to that ditzy girl you had to
work with on a group project. Maybe she was pretty, but she wasn't
very bright, and you could make fun of her to her face and she
wouldn't even realize it. Oh, you almost felt bad for her, except that
trying to get an A for your efforts was like taking one step forward
and two steps back thanks to her.

Example: This woman is saying so much nonsense, that's a
              complete moron.

              *Cette femme raconte tellement d'âneries, c'est un
              abruti fini.*

6. Cunt/Pussy/Twat: *Con/chatte*

Whether you need these words because some woman cut you in
line at the cafe or because your new French lover wants you to talk
dirty to her, it's best to have them memorized beforehand. That
pause as you pull out your little translation book just won't do!

Example: Despite her age, she had a very beautiful pussy.
              Malgré son âge elle avait une fort belle chatte.

7. Filthy bitch: *Pourriture*

How many variations on the word "bitch" does one person
need? An infinite amount. That's why you're so lucky this guide has

your back. If "slut" or "whore" just isn't descriptive enough, "filthy bitch" should do the trick, particularly if you have a little background on the object of your dislike, and you know what he or she is *really* like.

Example: This filthy bitch totally used me to his advantage.

Cette pourriture m'a complètement utilisée à son profit.

Insults for the Gentlemen

Men can be real jerks, can't they? And there are a lot of men running around France, so you'll want to be brushed up on your manly insults. You can say a lot of things to a guy, and he won't even bat an eyelash, so practicing how you string together these curse words would definitely add a certain panache to your vocabulary (and your personality!). Just remember: never insult a guy you can't outrun. We're not including any words like "help"; you're on your own there.

1. Motherfucker: *Enculé*

"Motherfucker" is quite the mack-daddy of insults, and while it can be — and often is — used as an exclamation ("Motherfucker!" you might say as you burn your tongue on a cup of coffee), we think it's best when hurled toward someone who has recently wronged you. But that's just one opinion. You can judge for yourself while you're in France.

Examples: This motherfucker has still not apologized for ruining the end-of-year party.
Cet enculé ne s'est toujours pas excusé d'avoir ruiné la soirée de fin d'année.

I can't trust him, he really looks like a real motherfucker.
Je n'arrive pas à lui faire confiance, il a quand même une belle tête d'enculé.

2. Asshole: *Connard*

There are a lot of euphemisms for "asshole," but if you want to call someone an asshole, just do it already. Don't go dancing around it all prissy-like. No one in America or France will respect you for it, and "connard" is just too fun to say.

Example: No need to talk to him, he's a first-class asshole.

Inutile de lui adresser la parole, c'est un connard de première.

3. Asshole: *Trou du cul*

Another great way to call someone an asshole is "trou du cul." French is really full of possibilities, isn't it?

Example: This is not a young asshole that will teach me my job!

Ce n'est pas un jeune trou du coup qui va m'apprendre mon métier!

4. Faggot: *Fiotte*

Nothing makes a person feel small like calling them a faggot, so even if it can be said in a loving, endearing sort of way, brandishing this insult toward someone whose guts you kinda, sorta, mostly hate — especially if they know you're an American by your accent — should shock them for at least a minute, giving you a distinct advantage.

Example: He always runs home to mummy, a genuine little faggot.

Toujours à se réfugier dans les jupes de sa mère, une vraie petite fiotte.

8

5. Fag/Faggot: *PD/Pédé/Pédéraste*

For a slight variation on the "faggot" theme, "pédéraste" and its equivalents (listed here) adds a more vile undertone to the concept, making it an even more narrow and zinging insult to accuse someone who is really getting on your nerves.

Example: I fought with Gérard, he called me a fag' just because I have long hair.

Je me suis battu avec Gérard, il m'a traité de pédé juste parce que j'ai les cheveux longs.

6. Bastard: *Bâtard*

It is understood that when you call someone a "bastard," you are generally not remarking on their parentage; you're simply pointing out what a dick they can be. However, if the object of your ire grew up in a French orphanage because his parents weren't married and they would have rather given him up for adoption than deal with his presence, well…savage. One hundred points to you.

Example: Fire her just before Christmas?! What a bastard!

La virer avant Noël ?! Quel bâtard!

7. Swine/Bastard: *Crevure*

For a porcine take on the classic "bastard" insult, see how "crevure" feels.

Example: What a bastard this guy, he leaves his wife and kids starving to death and blows all his cash in girls and booze!

*Quelle crevure ce mec, il laisse sa femme et ses gosses
crever la dalle et claques tout son fric en filles et en
alcool!*

8. Bastard: *Salaud*

For yet another twist, the word "salaud" is derived from
"salaude," a feminine word that has been replaced by slut. In this
instance, the word serves more as an adjective than a noun. But still,
it starts to make you wonder, doesn't it, that the French have three
words for "bastard"?

Example: That is really bastard what you've done.

C'est vraiment salaud ce que tu as fait là.

9. Real bastard: *Beau/vrai salaud*

Nothing is realer than the word "real," so if you stick it before
"bastard," it has to indicate a person of very low worth. This is a
nice phrase to memorize for those moments when you absolutely
must qualify the level of bastardry going on.

Example: I admit it; I happen to be a real bastard.

Je le reconnais, il m'arrive d'être un beau salaud.

10. Dastard/Bastard: *Saligaud*

Some bastards are indeed dastardly, to the level of a comic book
villain. For all the mustache-twirling villains you meet in France
(particularly the ones wearing effortlessly tilted berets), have
"saligaud" at the ready.

Example: The little dastard, he still made me a rotten trick.

Le petit saligaud, il m'a encore joué un tour pendable.

11. Dickhead: *Tête de nœud/de bite/de gland*

With a delightful precision and appreciation for the male anatomy "tête de gland" and its similar phrases have the effect of conveying the image of a penis head onto whomever you are speaking of. Here's a fun game: whenever you hear someone say "tête de gland" or "tête de bite" imagine a penis on that person's shoulders. Top it with their normal hair (if they have any). And then laugh!

Example: Some dickhead left his car in my space!

Une tête de nœud qui s'est garée sur ma place de parking!

14. Dickhead: *Con*

"Con" will appear several times in this guide, a testament to the French language's use of and reliance upon context and implication. Used correctly, "con" stands in for genital body parts in general and dickheads specifically at times.

Example: Just give up, he's such a dickhead.

Laisse tomber, il est vraiment trop con.

13. Degenerate: *Dégénéré*

Thanks to an incredibly similar spelling, the French word for "degenerate" should be easy to remember and recall, when you need it. This word is a bit fancy, even for French-speaking, so make sure you're using it among an audience who will appreciate your Shakespearean-level discourse.

Example: We're not necessarily safe from a degenerate man!

On est jamais à l'abri d'un dégénéré!

14. Wanker (UK)/Jerk (US): *Branleur*

"Wanker" (or "jerk" in American English) is a fairly common and general noun that is used often in all kinds of situations. Depending on how comfortable you are with those rolled Rs in French, you might find yourself reaching for "branleur" with equal frequency.

Example: Well, what a jerk this one!

Mais quel branleur celui-là!

15. Jackass: *Jean-foutre*

Americans have a slightly different take on the word "jackass," since the inception of the popular TV show; however, it's still going strong as a quick and easy put-down that doesn't cause too much emotional damage. "Foutre" here is actually slang for "fuck around"; with "Jean" attached the word "jackass" comes to mean "John do-nothing" or "generally useless fool" in French.

Example: They suck, a real team of jackasses.

Ils sont nuls, une véritable équipe de jean-foutre.

16. Old fart/Old schmuck: *Vieux con*

And here it is again! "Con" shows up for a third time, in this instance paired with the adjective "vieux." As perhaps the most versatile and common swear word, "con" usually takes its meaning based on whatever phrase it is part of, and that can vary from something extremely suggestive or vulgar to something less so, like "old fart."

Example: Try to become mature without turning into an old schmuck.

Essaye de devenir mature sans virer vieux con.

Equal-opportunity Insults, Slang Terms and Exclamations

1. To fuck somebody (in the ass): *Enculer quelqu'un*

Unless you get extremely lucky while you're in France, you will probably use this phrase only in the metaphorical sense — and hey, that's okay! This is a terrifically expressive phrase that livens up any complaint you might have while you're *en France*.

Example: I fucked him, I sold him the old one for the new price

Je l'ai bien enculé, je lui ai vendu l'ancien modèle au prix du nouveau.

2. Dork: *Blaireau*

When you think of French people you might assume they are all automatically very cool, cultured and sophisticated, but non — they have dorks, same as in the United States or anywhere else you go, for that matter. For every Olivier Martinez there are probably 10 Gerard Depardieus.

Example: This guy is just a dork!

C'est un vrai blaireau, ce mec!

3. Moron: *Imbécile*

Moron is another rather tame swear word by most standards, but when it is strung together with a few other choice expressions it can pack a decent punch. Actually, you should embrace the French version — "imbécile"— with all due enthusiasm, because it not only looks cool, it's a lot of fun to say. Go ahead, say it out loud a few times. The worst thing that can happen is you look like kind of a moron.

Example: This moron will again attract us problems.

Cet imbécile va encore nous attirer des problèmes.

4. Shit: *Merde*

Napoleon's military commander Pierre Cambronne supposedly uttered, "Merde," when the British demanded he surrender at the Battle of Waterloo in 1815. It has become an infamous legend for a rather infamous time, and while your usage of "merde" might not attain the same notoriety as Cambronne's, you hopefully won't be asked to surrender an army while you're visiting France, either.

Examples: There is always some dog shit on the pavement.

Il y a toujours une merde de chien sur le trottoir.

Stop buying crap.

Arrête d'acheter de la merde.

5. Fuck off/Go fuck yourself: *Aller se faire foutre/enculer*

Some people have a difficult time using their words, and they let their annoyance build and build until they snap. If you are one of those people, you might want to memorize the French for "go fuck yourself" or "fuck off," because nothing says, "I have reached my mortal limit" with quite such vehemence.

Example: If you don't like the sea, if you don't like the mountain, if you don't like the city...go fuck yourself!

Si vous n'aimez pas la mer, si vous n'aimez pas la montagne, si vous n'aimez pas la ville...allez vous faire foutre!

6. Ball-breaker: *Casse-burnes/casse-couilles*

If you're an agitator, the kind of person who just can't let something go without making a little comment or aside — especially when you know it will annoy the other person — you're what we call a ball-buster. You just like to bust people's balls. In French, that translates to "ball-breaker," but the sentiment is exactly the same.

Example: I hate to be a ball-breaker, but can I just do it?

Je déteste faire ma casse-couilles, mais est-ce que je peux le faire?

7. Tight-fisted: *Crevard*

We all have that one friend who is really, embarrassingly cheap. You don't even want to go out to dinner with them, because they ask you to split an appetizer with them, and shopping is horrific, because they try to use coupons that were expired a year ago. Well, if you make any new friends like that in France, you officially know what to call them!

Example: You're not even invited, you come empty-handed and emptied the fridge, you're a real tight-fisted jerk!

Tu n'es même pas invité, tu arrives les mains vides et en plus tu vides le frigo, quel crevard!

8. Fucking ("Whore of an"): *Putain*

Derived from the word for "whore," "putain" is a fun way of saying "fucking" that indicates the situation has really fucked you — you know, the way a sly whore would. Since "fuck" is such a versatile word in English, it's really interesting to see how the French language handles its variations, isn't it?

Example: A fucking update crashes the system!

Une putain de mise à jour a fait planter le système!

9. Pathetic loser: *Cas social/Cassos*

If you need to break up with someone while you're in France, calling them a "pathetic loser" in the French tongue at least sounds prettier than it does in English. Maybe it will help soften the blow, especially if you're dumping a significant other in the States?

Example: He's clueless: he doesn't live with his time, doesn't accept the reality … a pathetic loser.

C'est un paumé : il ne vit pas avec son temps, n'accepte pas la réalité… Un vrai cas social.

10. To be as stupid as fuck: *Être fini à la pisse*

When someone is "stupid as fuck," it is really satisfying to point it out for them, particularly in front of others. You're doing them a public service! Maybe they weren't aware of the fact, but now that they are, they can go do whatever it is fucking stupid people do to make themselves, well, less stupid.

Example: This guy is just stupid as fuck!

Ce mec est tellement stupide il a dû être fini à la pisse!

11. Someone who is whistling in the wind: *Enculeur de mouches*

In case you're unfamiliar, "whistling in the wind" refers to the act of trying to change or modify something in a situation where your attempt is clearly futile. (Literally whistling in the wind would be pointless, because the wind is a more powerful form of moving air that would envelope and negate your lovely lip music.)

Example: Well, perhaps it is time to stop whistling in the wind and start to work.

Bon, il serait peut-être temps d'arrêter de jouer aux enculeurs de mouches et de se mettre au travail.

12. Dirty trick/Low blow: *Coup de pute*

You know when someone hits "below the belt" during an argument? That's basically what "coup de pute" means, and it's a good phrase to keep in mind in case you're hot-headed and have a penchant for lashing out in cruel ways. You might hear someone use it to describe you, and it's not said in admiration.

Example: The bastard! That was a low blow!

Le salaud! Qui était un coup de pute!

13. Moron/Idiot: *Crétin*

Something as sophisticated-sounding as "crétin" should not stand in for "moron" or "idiot," but there you have it: the French language, making even the worst kinds of people sound as though they have some merit. Note, however, the similarities with the word "cretin" in English…all it takes is a little accent mark.

Example: That kid is a real moron.

Cet enfant est un vrai crétin.

14. To blow somebody: *Tailler une pipe à quelqu'un*

"Tailler" derives from the word for "prune," but another interpretation is "carve" — in this instance, "carve out" or make hollow. Blow jobs, "pipes" made hollow…do you see how this relates to getting head and the male anatomy? Let it not be said the French haven't any creativity (or a sense of humor, for that matter).

Example: You knew that Félix Faure, a former French president, died while his mistress was blowing him?

Tu savais que Félix Faure, un ancien président, était mort alors que sa maîtresse lui taillait une pipe?

15. Go to hell!: *Aller au diable*

Literally "Go with the devil," this phrase is a nice way of telling off someone who has started to get on your nerves and needs to take a step back. Maybe you want to add a little hand gesture, too, so the other person really knows they're being dismissed.

Example: Seriously, Guillaume, go to hell!

Sérieusement, Guillaume, va au diable!

16. Idiot: *Idiot*

What were you expecting? "Idioque" or something similarly impressive-looking? Nope, sorry. It's spelled exactly the same way, but unless you're texting it to someone, it will still come across with all the sass and brio for which the French are, rightfully, known.

Example: Jean is the village idiot.

Jean est l'idiot du village.

17. Dipstick/Nitwit: *Triple idiot*

Occasionally a person will come along who defies all logic and reason, at least in terms of how stupid they are. The things they say, compiled with the utterly ridiculous things they do, lead you to the conclusion that they are indeed a dipstick and/or a nitwit. And so, the French language has you covered.

Example: Can you stop doing stupid things, you nitwit!

Est-ce que tu peux arrêter de faire n'importe quoi, triple idiot!

18. Retard/Moron: *Débile*

Yes, there are retards and morons even in France, people being what they are (that is to say, consistent, around the world!). If you're in the capital city of Paris for any length of time and you happen to observe some of the traffic around you, well…it might be useful having "débile" at hand.

Example: I have enough of this retard and his nonsense.

J'en ai vraiment marre de ce débile et de ses débilités.

19. Half-wit: *Demeuré*

You can almost picture a proper English person saying, "Bloody half-wit!" at someone for whom they have a high level of disdain. It might not be quite as vulgar as some of the other phrases in this guide, but there is a time and place for everything, including "half-wit."

Example: Don't pay attention to him, he's a half-wit.

Ne prête pas attention à lui, c'est un demeuré.

20. Dumbass: *Abruti*

"Dumbass" and its translation "abruti" are great on their own, but when strung together with a few other choice insults —- such as "fucking" or "shit-face" — they really shine. Perfect for the guy or gal who is on their phone, not paying attention during a movie and bugging everyone around them.

Example: You have to be a dumbass to play soccer with a sprained ankle.

Il faut être un abruti pour jouer au foot avec une cheville foulée.

21. Dummy: *Neuneu*

"Dummy" is a nice term because it can be used across a wide variety of emotions, including anger, disappointment, resentment and even affection ("My dummy of a sister," you might sigh, after she drunk-dials you from the States and asks if she can crash at your place while you're abroad).

Example: He isn't mean, just a little dummy.

Il n'est pas méchant, il est juste un peu neuneu.

22. Look like a damn fool: *Passer pour un con*

You probably didn't feel particularly grateful to the last person who made you feel like a fool, but at least when you're in France you have this great little phrase to say, while shaking your fist at the sky, swearing retribution.

Example: Would you try to behave properly for once? Aren't you tired to look like a fool?

Tu ne voudrais pas te comporter correctement pour une fois ? N'en as-tu pas marre de passer pour un con ?

23. Damn lousy/bloody stupid: *À la con*

À la con, indeed! How do the French take something dripping with such disdain and make it sound so fancy and melodious? Answer: it's what they do. They could tell you they're screwing your mother and it would sound pretty.

Example: I'm sick of your damn lousy remarks!

Ras le bol de tes remarques à la con!

24. Scum: *Ordure*

When was the last time you used the word "scum"? It has fallen out of usage in the last 15 or so years, but that just means it's time to bring it back. If anyone asks, your use of "*ordure*" is vintage!

Example: In that case, he behaved like a scum.

Dans cette affaire, il s'est conduit comme une ordure.

25. Riffraff: *Racaille*

Riffraff is actually more charming than insulting, another word that invokes the feeling of a different, bygone era. If you have any French kids to yell at — maybe they need to get the hell off your lawn — "racaille" should do the trick.

Example: This band of riffraff yet tried to extort me a few bucks.

Cette bande de racailles a encore cherché à me soutirer quelques billets.

26. Crook: *Canaille*

If you can make the time to find an open-air market in France, you absolutely should, and you might want to take "canaille" with you, too, just in case some huckster tries to pull the wool over your eyes.

Example: He behaved like a vile crook.

Il s'est conduit comme une vile canaille.

Made in the USA
San Bernardino, CA
16 January 2017